D0185731

Food around the world

India

Polly Goodman

WAYLAND

First published in Great Britain in 2006 by Wayland,
an imprint of Hachette Children's Books

Hachette Children's Books
338 Euston Road, London NW1 3BH

Copyright © 2006 Wayland

The right of Polly Goodman to be identified as
the author of this work as been asserted by her
in accordance with the Copyright, Designs and Patents
Act, 1988.

All rights reserved. Apart from any use permitted under
UK copyright law, this publication may only be
reproduced, stored or transmitted, in any form, or by
any means with prior permission in writing of the
publishers or in the case of reprographic production in
accordance with the terms of licences issued by the
Copyright Licensing Agency.

Editor: Sarah Gay
Senior Design Manager: Rosamund Saunders
Designer: Tim Mayer
Consultant: Susannah Blake

Printed and bound in China

British Library Cataloguing in Publication Data
Goodman, Polly
    India. - (Food around the world)
    1.Food habits - India - Juvenile literature 2.Cookery,
    Indic - Juvenile literature 3.India - Social life and
    customs - Juvenile literature
    I.Title
    394.1'2'0954

ISBN-10: 0-7502-4897-1
ISBN-13: 978-0-7502-4897-6

SCOTTISH BORDERS LIBRARY SERVICE	
007299627	
CAW	07/12/2006
J394.1209	£11.99

Cover photograph: an Indian man selling spices on
the street.

Photo credits: Richard I'Anson/Lonely Planet 6, 10, 22
and 23, Lindsay Brown/Lonely Planet 8, Chris
Beall/Lonely Planet 9, Greg Elms/Lonely Planet 11 and
21, Paul Beinssen/Lonely Planet 12, Lee Studios/Anthony
Blake Photo Library 13 and 26, Dallas Stribley/Lonely
Planet 14, Fabfoodpix 15, Wayland Picture Library 16
and title page, Catherine Karnow/CORBIS 17, Stuart
Freedman/Panos Pictures 18, foodfolio/Alamy 19,
Eaglemoss Consumer Publications/Anthony Blake Photo
Library 20, Dinodia Photo Library 24, DANISH
ISMAIL/Reuters/Corbis 25, Frans Lemmens/zefa/Corbis
cover.

The website addresses (URLs) included in this book
were valid at the time of going to press. However,
because of the nature of the Internet, it is possible that
some addresses may have changed, or sites may have
changed or closed down since publication. While the
author and publisher regret any inconvenience this may
cause the readers, no responsibility for any such changes
can be accepted by either the author or the publisher.

Contents

Words in **bold** can be found in the glossary on page 28

Welcome to India

India is a huge country in Asia. It is famous for its hot, spicy food. Religion is very important in India. It affects what people eat. Most people in India are Hindus, but there are many other religions, including Muslims, Sikhs, Christians and Buddhists.

▼ The busy Ganges river in northern India is very important to Hindus.

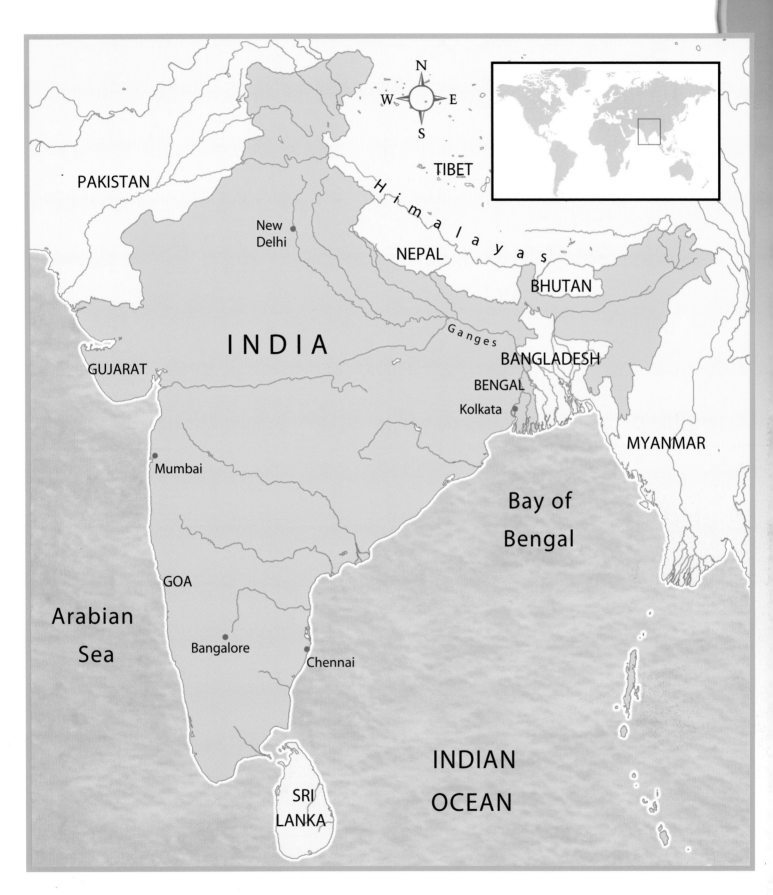

▲ India is marked on this map in orange.
It is 13 times bigger than the UK.

Farming and weather

India stretches over 5,600 km, from the Himalayas in the north to the Indian Ocean in the south. Some foods grow well in the cool mountains of northern India. Other foods grow well in the hot, tropical south.

▼ *Tea grows well in the hot, wet weather of southern India.*

In northern India, wheat grows well on the **fertile** plains around the Ganges and Indus rivers. Further south, rice, spices and many tropical fruits are suited to the hotter, wetter weather.

▲ *Winnowing wheat in northern India.*

SCOTTISH BORDERS COUNCIL

LIBRARY & INFORMATION SERVICES

Food fact

Spices come from different plants, such as the capsicum bush, ginger plant and clove tree.

Bread, rice and spices

Wheat is ground and made into many different breads. **Pappadams** and **pooris** are fried. **Naans** are cooked in an oven. **Parathas** are flatbreads that are stuffed with potatoes or other fillings. People in India use bread to scoop up their food.

▼ All sorts of bread are for sale outside this bakery in northern India.

▲ This dish, called vegetable pilau, is made from rice, spices and vegetables.

Food fact

Spices make food taste and smell good, and some help the body with **digestion**.

Rice is cooked in different ways. Pilau is a rice dish flavoured with spices and stock. Rice fried with meat, fish or vegetables is called a biryani. Ground rice is made into rice cakes, called **idlis**.

Vegetables, pulses and fruit

There are hundreds of vegetable dishes in India. Many include lentils, chickpeas, kidney beans or other **pulses**. Lentils are cooked with spices to make a sauce called daal. Other vegetables are fried in chickpea batter to make **samosas** or **bhajis**.

◀ Bhajis, samosas and spicy crisps for sale at a market stall.

Tropical fruits such as mangoes and **papaw** are made into chutneys. They are served as side dishes. Cucumber and other vegetables are mixed with yoghurt to make a dish called a **raita**.

▲ *This raita contains yoghurt, cucumber, pepper, mint and onion.*

Food fact

It's nice and cooling to eat a raita after a hot, spicy dish.

Fish and meat

In coastal towns and villages in India, **pomfret**, mackerel and other fresh fish are caught and eaten. Bummalo fish are small fish that are dried and made into a dish called **Bombay Duck**. Prawns, mussels and lobsters are also popular.

◄ *Women in Mumbai sort the catch of the day into different types of fish.*

Lamb and chicken are the most popular meats in India. Lamb is often cubed, **marinated** and cooked on a skewer, called a kebab. Tandoori chicken is marinated in yoghurt and spices, then cooked in a clay oven, called a tandoor.

▲ Rogan Josh is a curry usually made with lamb, tomatoes and spices.

Shopping and street food

Food in India is mostly bought fresh from local markets. Most villages have a bakery, fishmonger, butcher, and a general store selling rice, drinks and tinned foods. Some of the larger towns also have supermarkets.

▼ Chutneys and spices for sale at a market stall.

Street vendors cook and sell pooris, samosas, **bhelpuris** and other snacks from roadside stalls. Some serve fresh, tropical fruit juices, and a traditional Indian yoghurt drink called **lassi**.

▲ Lassi is made from yoghurt, water, salt and spices.

Mealtimes in India

Everyday Indian meals might include dishes from the menus below.

Breakfast

Paratha (pancake stuffed with cheese or vegetables)

Idlis (rice cakes) and a bowl of sambar (spicy soup)

Water

Tea

▼ These men are delivering hot lunch boxes to office workers in the city.

Lunch

Thali (metal tray) containing the following:

Dhal

Okra bhaji (spicy okra)

Matar panir (cheese and peas in a spicy sauce)

Raita potatoes (potatoes and yoghurt)

Pickles & chutneys

Rice

Chapatis (flatbreads)

Water

Banana lassi

Dinner

Rice

Spicy pulses

Potatoes

Chapatis (flatbreads)

Dosas (pancakes)

Fresh fruit

▶ *A thali meal.*

Around the country

There are different cooking styles all over India. In northern India and in Muslim areas, people eat mainly meat, vegetables and breads. Spicy lamb dishes such as Rogan Josh are common.

▼ Tandoori Chicken comes from northern India.

In the south, fish is eaten on the coast and rice is part of every meal. Southern dishes often contain tropical fruits and nuts, such as coconut, mangoes and cashew nuts. In areas with strict Hindus, such as Gujarat, most people are **vegetarian**.

▲ Dosas are pancakes made from rice and lentil flour. They come from southern India.

Special occasions

Indians celebrate important events with special meals. At a Hindu wedding, the guests enjoy a huge feast with over 20 different dishes, including desserts such as kheer (rice pudding) and kulfi (ice cream).

▼ At a Hindu wedding, rice and rose petals are thrown to wish the bride and groom good luck.

When Sikhs go to the temple, they share a meal together in the langer (kitchen). Everyone helps to prepare and serve the food. At a Sikh wedding, a special sweet called **karah prashad** is blessed and passed around before everyone shares a meal.

▲ In this Sikh temple, everyone helps peel potatoes for a shared meal.

Festival food

The biggest festival in India is Diwali. It is celebrated by both Hindus and Sikhs. People take gifts of sweets to friends and relatives. They might take jalebis (fried sweets), gulab jamuns (fried milk balls) or barfi (milk fudge).

▼ These plates of barfi and other sweets are ready for Diwali.

◄ Muslims pray together before breaking their fast during Ramadan.

During the month of Ramadan, Muslims **fast** during the hours of daylight. Id-ul-Fitr celebrates the end of Ramadan, and families eat a big lunch together. They eat sweet foods such as dates, almonds and cakes.

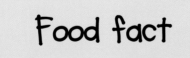

Food fact

After sunset, Muslims break their Ramadan fast by eating a special meal called Ifthar.

Make a mixed raita!

What you need

300g plain yoghurt

1 tablespoon fresh mint leaves

1 small cucumber

1 red pepper

$\frac{1}{2}$ onion

$\frac{1}{4}$ teaspoon ground nutmeg

What to do

1. Put the yoghurt into a bowl.

2. Chop the mint, cucumber, pepper and onion and add them to the yoghurt.

3. Mix everything together with the nutmeg and serve.

4. Decorate with mint leaves.

Ask an adult help you make this dish. Always be careful with sharp knives.

A balanced diet

This food pyramid shows which foods you should eat to have a healthy, **balanced diet**.

We shouldn't eat too many fats, oils, cakes or sweets.

Milk, cheese, meat, fish, beans and eggs help to keep us strong.

We should eat plenty of vegetables and fruit to keep healthy.

Bread, cereal, rice and pasta should make up most of our diet.

Indian meals use all foods from the pyramid. Some Indian dishes are fried in oil but most Indian meals are balanced because they contain rice or bread with vegetables, meat or fish.

Glossary

balanced diet a diet that includes a mixture of different foods, which supply all the things a body needs to keep healthy

bhaji deep-fried vegetables in batter

bhelpuri a snack made from lentil-flour noodles, puffed rice and wheat crackers with diced, boiled potatoes and chutneys

Bombay Duck a dish made from dried bummalo fish

digestion the process of breaking down food in the body

fast to go without food

fertile land that is good for growing crops

idlis rice cakes

karah prashad a sweet-tasting pudding made from semolina, sugar and butter, that has been blessed

lassi a drink made from yoghurt

marinated soaked in a sauce to add flavour

naan a thick, baked flatbread

papaw a fruit with orange flesh and small black seeds

pappadam an Indian flatbread made from lentil flour

paratha flatbreads that is often stuffed with a variety of fillings

poori crispy, puffed-up, deep-fried bread

pomfret a saltwater fish

pulses beans, peas and other foods that are edible seeds

raita a side dish made from yoghurt, onion and mint

samosa deep-fried pastry containing spiced vegetables or meat

vegetarian a person who does not eat meat or fish

winnowing blowing air through wheat to separate the good bits from the bad bits

Further information

Books to read

A Flavour of India by Mike Hirst (Wayland, 2001)

Ceremonies and Celebrations: Feasts and Fasting by Kerena Marchant (Wayland, 2001)

Fiesta! India by S. Dawson (Watts, 2001)

Kids Around the World Celebrate!: The Best Feasts and Festivals from Many Lands by Lynda Jones (John Wiley & Sons, 2000)

Let's Eat! What Children Eat Around the World by Beatrice Hollyer (Frances Lincoln, 2003)

Letters from Around the World: India by David Cumming (Cherrytree Books, 2002)

Picture a Country: India by Henry Pluckrose (Watts, 2001)

A World of Recipes: India by Julie McCulloch (Heinemann, 2001)

Websites

CIA Factbook

www.cia.gov/cia/publications/factbook

Facts and figures about Italy and other countries.

About.com

http://indianfood.about.com

Information and recipes for Indian dishes.

Index

SCOTTISH BORDERS COUNCIL

LIBRARY &
INFORMATION SERVICES